Thoughtless Poems of a Thoughtful Mind

G. E. Truman

BookLeaf Publishing

India | USA | UK

Presentation by *BookLeaf Publishing*

Web: www.bookleafpub.com

E-mail: info@bookleafpub.com

ISBN: 9789358311822

First edition 2023

*I dedicate this book to the younger me, who
never saw this [life] coming.*

Relish in it.

ACKNOWLEDGEMENT

I profess my deep gratitude for each person in my life- stranger or family- that have encouraged me, supported me, or simply brought about more musings.

I am thankful to BookLeaf Publishing for the incredible opportunity to publish my debut book- thank you.

PREFACE

These poems are mere thoughts I needed to put on a page. Everything from Unwritten by Natasha Bedingfield to Iris by the Goo Goo Dolls have inspired me during my long drives into a day job.

Through this short book of the feelings and thoughts I've gathered through an also short life, I have been able to do more of what I love so deeply than I ever have before.

First you should know,

I'm a writer but the amount of blank pages haunting me says otherwise. But I promise you she's there. Burdened beneath piles of papers and bills, small talk and sleep deprivation, a writer within me both pushes me forward, and sometimes pushes me right into a deep, dark well. Sometimes I feel rock bottom and think, at least I know I'm there. Sometimes I don't see walls or the bottom, and I know if I were to drop something I would not hear water and I would not hear my pen hitting the stone.

I'm a writer but there's all these people shooting blanks into the air and though I don't want to run, I'm not ready to run and already out of breath, I run. And run and run and run. Usually only fluorescent lights and email notifications stop me.

I'm a writer but then textbooks burn themselves into my blue irises, and I will often imagine lying flat in a field while my lungs face a blue sky and fluffy white clouds. I can feel green blades trying to cut themselves on my sensitive skin and wind rushing through my eyelashes, through my chest. Day in and day out I actively choose not to give the writer what she needs; air, space, earth, quiet. A good game paired with a crime series, the concentrate of weed to make up for my lack thereof, and chocolate are "all a girl needs". It is a hard offer to pass up, but one that I must exchange for the outpouring of words and feelings and vomit that boil in my flesh.

I'm a writer, and I can feel a sigh of relief. I lost sleep, but now the writer rests.

good things come to those who wait

I think about you
the way I think about anything that is
so good
you must wait for it for a
very
very
very
long time.
the way something so good
is always
so worth
the wait

some nights
I think the wait
must be longer than a
heavy heart and
thin skin
can endure

about shared experience

on things like
global news or
the weather
we will commiserate

when we must all stand
together in rain
or trudge together in snow
we will unite

but when I am drenched
poured over
and cold
others will remain dry
and commiserate about that

swimming on a beach on an island in a fish bowl

it is uncomfortable
how I spill with anguish
overwhelmed
body sweats
bleeds
swells

how I crumble with apathy
eyes drift
mind drifts
I drift

somewhere far away
I'm awake
and alive
I sweat
from the heat
I bleed
because I'm living
feeling

I swell with excitement and ferocity
I am not drifting
unless of course across the sea

in this beautiful
beautiful
fish
bowl

relapse

you're sad and hateful
in moments that the earth shakes
you tremble and
you wonder if death is on the table again.

weird how the earth settles
so quickly your trembles
grow tired and
you fall in line and
death's bed is
not the one you're sleeping in
for now

beagle

you look up at me
with the eyes
of a hundred lives
and a soul
deeper than mine

jaded

wouldn't you just love that
to be engorged with art and music and soul and
wonder if you had the time or the
space or the energy if inspiration
would feed your deepest most constant hunger
or
would inspiration just eat you for itself
souped up in all your unused potential and
spit you back out and
wonder if you'd still be growing up
jaded

march

tried to sleep in the rain
last night
wanted to get some real rest
lately I've just noticed the fatigue
it's gloomy
but mostly
I notice how heavy everything is
my arms, my hands
moving one foot in front of the other
even my heart
labors in each pump-
da-
-almost-
doosh.
da-
-heavy still-
doosh.

I think I'll have to close my eyes now
and chances are I'll wake up again.
not that I mind really
but I will still awake with the hope that
the car will drive itself and
paper will push itself and

well I'm rambling,
I do tend to do that

I hope you sleep
well.

inner thoughts

impulsive or intrusive
I'm not sure
I just want to pour this cold water on me
shock the system
I just want to put my head through this wall
then regret it
I just want to pull this steering wheel
shout out the shit in my head
to this store
dig my nails deep into this skin
ambush my nerves
throw this glass at the wall and
photograph the shattered mosaic
I just want to scream until the veins in this face
are pulsating
swelling
popping

in case you were wondering
I won't actually do those things
and neither will you
we will both just keep imagining
until we don't

something about all this
doesn't seem real

getting older makes
my body seem
both
more mortal
and less
like
me
as time passes I
begin to question
was time ever really
real

I can tell that I am
alive
or at least not
dead
but where
did
I
actually
go

nauseated on a ship at sea

as if to tell me
it was not time to awake
dreams continued
in the middle of my room
as I swam through shadows
and navigated old laundry
old me in this body
it was all I could do to
close my eyes and
hit the ground
running

fleeting

wondering if
if it is
the exuberance
the joy
my giddy organs
that are fleeting or
is it that
anguish that
agony that
makes me so
incredibly
insatiable that
is the
fleeting
part
of me

just ahead

the music stopped working
in the car
and so I approached the stationary cars
ahead
baby on board lets off the break
but then
stopped again

with the music lost
and window open
I began to wonder if Friday morning traffic
had always marched
past me
somberly
steadily

baby on board makes a move
I make the opposite
finally I am free to
cruise along this road but
then
Connecticut Suburban crawls
this is unacceptable
don't you know what is waiting for me
Connecticut

Suburban makes a move
I make the opposite
agility guides me through a spiraling road
must not distract from
what's ahead

finally I am in a building
race past colleagues
worried I must look
crazy
but more worried
I will lose what's
coming

I just know there is
something here
waiting
just
ahead

the turtle the cat and a
homeless man

why do we care so much
for the turtle stuck in the road
the stray cats that visit us
there are plenty of turtles and plenty cats
if one dies or
ceases to exist
there will be another turtle crossing or
another cat approaching
cautiously

I think it's for the same reason
we care for our brothers and sisters
mothers and fathers and children and friends and
the poor homeless man you pass while driving
your car

my brother and sister and
mother and father and child and friend
could be the ones omitted from
your compassion

I continue to care for the turtle and the cat
the homeless man
even if there will always be more
where they came from

remember middle school?

many of my days have
passed me by without a second
thought though
years and years later
a yellowed memory of
sixth grade study hall
makes me question just how many days
are lost on me

sixth grade reminds me of all the ages I wished
to be
twelve meant lockers
sixteen meant driving-
freedom
eighteen meant adulthood
but did it?
twenty-one meant I could go to a bar
but did I?
twenty-five meant lower rates on car insurance
which I did not find to be the case anyway
and now that
twenty-six is upon me
I have yet to find the next desirable age
is it
the one where I'm making more

money
the one where I'm buying a
house a
car and having a
family

that study hall was strange
the teacher seemed to admire how I did not part
take in the
obnoxious
overstimulating antics in the back rather
attempted lettering with my non-dominate hand
the left and
wrote notes to myself and
occasionally looked out the window
for a long time until the bell rang or
one of those rowdy kids threw their pencil past
me
almost as quick as that day passed

to whatever song is playing

how is it that
I fill days with paper and
papers
emails and
miles and miles
and yet any hour that does not
overstimulate
overwhelm
reminds me of the void
that I exist
within
I do not have the time
or do I
for the things that would
maybe
fill
some
of the
empty

pleasantries

would you like that toasted?
yes please
that'll be five sixty-six
thank you, keep the change
oh you didn't have to do that..
not a problem
thank you

I'm sorry
you can go ahead of me
oh that's okay
are you sure?
oh yeah
don't worry
I get paid by the hour
laughs

doing anything fun this weekend?
you know
the usual
and you?
well my brother's girlfriend's sister
is having a baby
there is a shower
oh

lovely
yes well
have a great night
weekend I mean
have a great weekend!
enjoy the shower!

oh you went to Mexico?
lovely
parties?
sounds fun!

I couldn't force myself
to speak aloud
even to myself
in the car
alone on the way
home
I silently lose track of music
traffic
and soon enough I
wake up home

I'm going to stand still for a moment

breathe

I can
not

remember

how it

felt

when
b r e a t h i n g

came

easily.

more I

remember

going
going

going

while
b r e a t h i n g

just
happened.

messy

blankets lie lazily
morose
around me
mom calls me

the dog lies lazily
downhearted
next to me
dad talks to me

I notice the room is dark
and I say to mom
"I need space"
quickly
she replies

"okay"
I'm left with the pleasure
of closure with
the absence
of resolve

hometown

even out here in this country
the way that sparkly car
glistens in subtle hometown
gas station lights reminds me of
those times in the city
so impressed by how metropolitan the
shimmer of lights can be
with all the noise and pedestrians
so
here in these grassy
dusty
lonely roads
a shimmering car reminds me of some kind of a
world
some kind of a hope

happy new year

days where time is not
standing
still
not
moving
quickly

discovery of self lies
somewhere
time does
not
reach

I've noticed the time for the first time
on the first day
of this year
I saw how remnants of my
discoveries rest
with ease

I am taken by
the lack of
tension
and I am
given

explicit
direction
by self
to bask
in it.